Creative Company Direct 1/19/07 $27.10

THE STORY OF THE
MINNESOTA
TIMBERWOLVES

CREATIVE EDUCATION

Published by Creative Education
123 South Broad Street
Mankato, Minnesota 56001
Creative Education is an imprint of The Creative Company.

DESIGN AND PRODUCTION BY **EVANSDAY DESIGN**

PHOTOGRAPHS BY Getty Images (Gary Bassing / NBAE, Andrew
D. Bernstein / NBAE, Lisa Blumenfeld, Tim Defrisco, Andy Hayt /
NBAE, Kent Horner / NBAE, Glenn James / NBAE, David Liam Kyle
/ NBAE, Ken Levine / Allsport, Melissa Majchrzak, Robert Mora /
NBAE, Doug Pensinger / Allsport, Ryan / Beyer, David Sherman
/ NBAE, Todd Warshaw / Allsport)

LIBRARY OF CONGRESS CATALOGING-IN-PUBLICATION DATA

Gilbert, Sara.
The story of the Minnesota Timberwolves / by Sara Gilbert.
p. cm. — (The NBA—a history of hoops)
Includes index.
ISBN-13: 978-1-58341-415-6
1. Minnesota Timberwolves (Basketball team)—History—
Juvenile literature. I. Title. II. Series.

GV885.52.M565G55 2006
796.323'64'097795759—dc22   2005051200

First edition

9 8 7 6 5 4 3 2 1

COVER PHOTO: *Kevin Garnett*

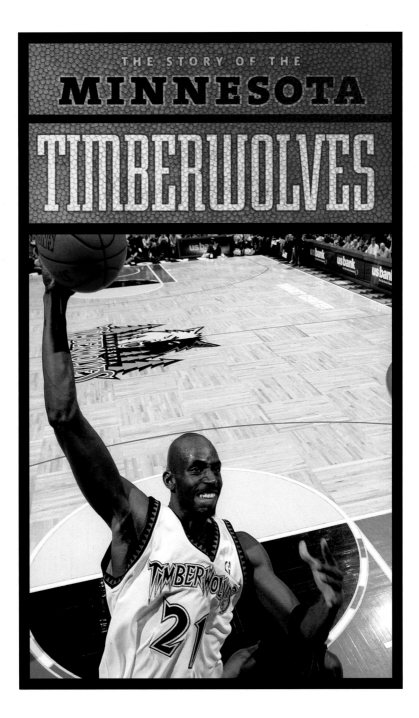

THE STORY OF THE

MINNESOTA

TIMBERWOLVES

SARA GILBERT

CREATIVE C EDUCATION

The Minnesota Timberwolves'

KEVIN GARNETT LOOKS LIKE A HUMAN EXCLAMATION POINT AS HE DRIVES TOWARD THE BASKET. THE WIRY, 6-FOOT-11 FORWARD LEAPS TOWARD THE BASKET, HIS LONG LEGS PROPELLING HIM ABOVE THE CROWD OF OPPONENTS BELOW. HE TWISTS HIS BODY IN MIDAIR AND JAMS THE BALL THROUGH THE HOOP, THE MUSCLES IN HIS ARMS GLISTENING WITH THE EFFORT. AS THE TARGET CENTER CROWD IN MINNEAPOLIS CHEERS WILDLY, GARNETT OPENS HIS MOUTH IN AN ALMOST PERFECT "O" AND LETS OUT A HOWL THAT SEEMS TO EMANATE FROM SOMEWHERE DEEP IN THE TIMBER OF MINNESOTA'S NORTH WOODS.

MINNESOTA TIMBERWOLVES
Twin Cities Minnesota

MINNEAPOLIS AND SAINT PAUL ARE KNOWN AS Minnesota's "Twin Cities." Divided by the mighty Mississippi River, the two communities—and towns throughout Minnesota—share a love of the outdoors. Whether camping, boating, or fishing, people in the "Land of 10,000 Lakes" enjoy being out among the elements.

Outdoor enthusiasts can sometimes hear the howl of one of Minnesota's defining creatures echoing through the state's northern forests. In 1989, when the National Basketball Association (NBA) granted Minnesota a new team, it seemed only natural to name the franchise after one of the state's best-known predators—the Timberwolves.

9

TIMBERWOLVES

Tony Campbell was the first-year Timberwolves' most dangerous scorer, averaging 23 points a game

10

Selected with the Wolves' first-ever NBA Draft pick, Pooh Richardson played three seasons in Minnesota

The first Wolves were mostly players that other teams had released, and team officials knew they needed a coach who could squeeze the maximum amount of effort out of each player. They found their man in Bill Musselman, a former University of Minnesota coach known for his ability to motivate players. "It's great to be here," Musselman said in his gruff style. "Now let's build a winner."

Although guard Sidney Lowe and forwards Sam Mitchell, Tony Campbell, and Brad Lohaus shared their coach's affinity for hard work, physical play, and stubborn defense, victories were scarce for Minnesota in 1989–90, and the team finished 22–60 playing in the cavernous Hubert H. Humphrey Metrodome.

The next season, the Wolves moved into the brand-new Target Center, and young point guard Jerome "Pooh" Richardson helped Minnesota improve to 29–53. Unfortunately, the team faltered again the following year under new head coach Jimmy Rodgers, posting a miserable 15–67 record.

McHALE IN MINNESOTA

Kevin McHale grew up in Hibbing, on Minnesota's Iron Range. At 6-foot-10, the barrel-chested forward was a natural on the basketball court, and he became legendary for his polished inside game during his Hall of Fame career with the Boston Celtics. When he retired in 1993, McHale joined the Timberwolves' front office, eventually working his way up to vice president of basketball operations. Midway through the 2004–05 season, he also briefly took over as coach after firing longtime friend Flip Saunders, the winningest coach in franchise history. "I'm going to do the best I can," McHale said. "I'm going to try and instill some confidence in our guys and get some swagger back." The Wolves went 19–12 under McHale but missed the playoffs only a year after recording the NBA's best record.

LOOKING TO LAETTNER

THE WOLVES' POOR RECORD HELPED THEM SECURE the third overall pick in the NBA Draft in 1992. With it, they chose Christian Laettner, a 6-foot-11 and 240-pound center from Duke University. The Wolves also traded for sharpshooting forward Chuck "The Rifleman" Person and point guard Michael Williams. Still, the team remained at the bottom of the Midwest Division, and Rodgers was fired at midseason.

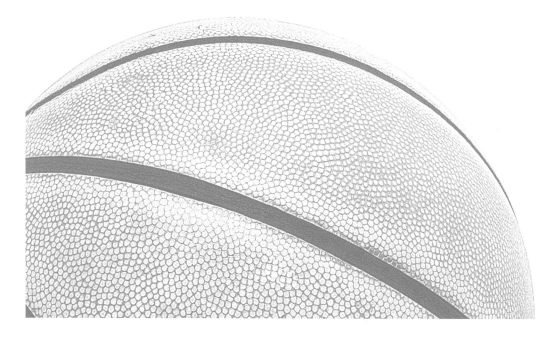

13

TIMBERWOLVES

Christian Laettner was one of the most famous college players of all time before entering the NBA in 1992

14

Forward Tom Gugliotta became a fan favorite in Minnesota due to his unselfish and hardworking playing style

The Wolves hired Sidney Lowe, the team's former point guard, to replace Rodgers as coach. But the losses continued to pile up. Minnesota won only 19 games in 1992–93 and 20 the following year. Except for Laettner and shooting guard Isaiah Rider, the team's top pick in the 1993 NBA Draft, the Timberwolves' roster consisted mostly of journeymen and aging veterans.

Laettner and Rider struggled to carry the franchise at such young ages. Rider was an explosive scorer, but he was also wildly inconsistent in both his play and behavior. Laettner, meanwhile, grew frustrated by the team's woes. "The losing just turns you numb after a while," he said. "I lost more games here in a month than I did my whole college career."

During the 1994–95 season, the Timberwolves' erratic play nearly led the team to be sold and moved to New Orleans. When the NBA vetoed the sale, the team was instead sold to local businessman Glen Taylor. Taylor soon added talented forward Tom Gugliotta to the roster, but Minnesota still set an NBA record with a fourth straight season of at least 60 losses.

RIDER TO THE RIM

The Timberwolves were still a relatively new team when they hosted the 1994 NBA All-Star Weekend in Minneapolis. But they were ready to shine the spotlight on their new home, the Target Center, and on their flashy rookie guard, Isaiah Rider. Rider did not disappoint the hometown crowd. He dazzled the Target Center crowd with his performance in the Slam Dunk Contest, winning with a between-the-legs slam he called the "East Bay Funk Dunk." At the time, Houston Rockets forward Charles Barkley said Rider's slam "might be the best dunk I've ever seen." Although Rider's erratic behavior off the court shortened his stay with the Wolves to just three seasons and his NBA career to just nine rocky years, that dunk remains one of the most memorable moments of the team's early years.

IN 1995, FORMER BOSTON CELTICS STAR KEVIN McHale took over the Timberwolves' basketball operations. McHale had won three NBA championships with the Celtics, and he hoped to breathe life into the luckless Wolves. "We're officially out of excuses," McHale said. "Our fans have been patient. Now we have to give them something to get excited about."

McHale's first move was a brilliant one, selecting high school phenom Kevin Garnett with the fifth overall pick in the 1995 NBA Draft. The 6-foot-11 Garnett appeared to be the impact player the Wolves needed, but to ensure that he developed at his own pace, the Wolves hired McHale's good friend (and former college teammate at the University of Minnesota) Phil "Flip" Saunders as the new head coach. In 1995–96, the team went an improved 26–56.

TIMBERWOLVES

Nicknamed "Da Kid" and "The Big Ticket," Kevin Garnett wasted no time in becoming the Wolves' first superstar

18

Stephon Marbury used incredible quickness and explosive leaping ability to take the ball to the basket

The next year, the Timberwolves jumped to 40–42 and gave Minnesota fans their first taste of postseason basketball. Leading the way was Garnett, who replaced the departed Laettner as a team leader and averaged 17 points, 8 rebounds, and 2 blocked shots per game. "That kid is the future of basketball," said Houston Rockets All-Star forward Charles Barkley. "He says he's 6-foot-11, but he's a 7-footer who can run, jump, and play all three of the frontcourt positions."

But Garnett didn't carry the team alone. The 1996–97 Wolves also had a new weapon in lightning-quick point guard Stephon Marbury, and Gugliotta netted 20 points per game. Hardworking center Dean Garrett and guard Doug West, meanwhile, gave the team a pair of quality defensive stoppers. The young Wolves were swept from the 1997 playoffs by the veteran Houston Rockets, but they were finally howling.

POOF OF POWDER

Sportswriters covering the Minnesota Timberwolves know what to expect from All-Star Kevin Garnett just before tip-off. As the other players are taking the court, the playful forward fills one of his enormous palms with talcum powder, leans over the media table, and claps his hands together, releasing a cloud of powder that covers the reporters' faces, computers, coffee cups, and anything else in the vicinity. Although Wolves fans love the ritual and local reporters tolerate the inconvenience, scorers and members of the media for the opposing team are sometimes startled by the unexpected shower. The ritual is reminiscent of the pre-game routine of NBA legend Michael Jordan, who would often sprinkle the Chicago Bulls radio announcer with the sweat-absorbing powder with a clap of his hands before taking the floor.

THE TIMBERWOLVES POSTED THEIR FIRST WINNING record in 1997–98. Marbury's attacking offensive style blended perfectly with Garnett's ability to run the floor and finish off fast breaks. The Wolves finished the regular season 45–37 and pushed the heavily favored Seattle SuperSonics to five games before bowing out in the first round of the playoffs.

Unfortunately, before the start of the next season, Minnesota's promising core was dismantled. Gugliotta left town as a free agent, and Marbury demanded a trade and was dealt to the New Jersey Nets. They were replaced by forward Joe Smith and veteran point guard Terrell Brandon. Garnett, Smith, and Brandon carried the team back into the playoffs in 1999, but Minnesota fell to the eventual NBA champion San Antonio Spurs in the first round.

21

Known for his smart and steady play, Terrell Brandon led Minnesota in assists for three straight seasons

NBA

22

Joe Smith contributed 10 points a game and was a valuable rebounder during his four years in Minnesota

In 1999, Minnesota drafted forward Wally Szczerbiak, who could either light it up from three-point range or slash his way to the basket. Szczerbiak and swingman Malik Sealy helped the more balanced Timberwolves record their best record yet in 1999–00, a 50–32 mark. Minnesota quickly fell to the powerful Portland Trail Blazers in the playoffs, but harsher blows were yet to come.

A few weeks after the playoff loss, Sealy was killed in a car accident. Then, the NBA ruled that Joe Smith and the Wolves had held secret, illegal contract negotiations. NBA Commissioner David Stern levied a large fine on the team, took away Minnesota's next five first-round picks in the annual NBA Draft, and forced Smith to leave the team. Amazingly, despite all of this adversity, the 2000–01 Timberwolves raced back into the playoffs, falling in the first round.

In 2001, Smith returned to the Wolves' roster, and the team won 50 games, including a record-setting, 53-point victory over the Chicago Bulls in November. But the team couldn't maintain that momentum in the post-season, and the Dallas Mavericks swept Minnesota in the first round. Wolves fans wondered if things would ever change.

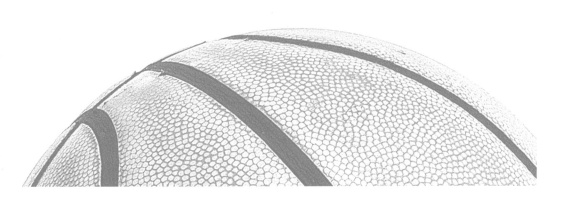

24

Although not a terrific defender, forward Wally Szczerbiak was one of the purest shooters in the NBA

A LASTING LOSS

Wolves swingman Malik Sealy was out celebrating teammate Kevin Garnett's 24th birthday on the evening of May 20, 2000. He finally headed home in the wee hours of the morning, driving on a highway near Minneapolis, but a drunk driver going the wrong way crashed into Sealy's vehicle head-on, killing him. Sealy, who had joined the Timberwolves as a free agent in 1999, was popular with players and fans alike, both for his hardworking approach to basketball and his honest approach to life. His death left a gaping hole on the team. "I don't think anybody has anything that's going to make anything better with the situation," said Kevin McHale, the team's vice president of basketball operations. "There's a huge sense of loss and a huge sense of just sadness."

POSTSEASON PROGRESS

WHEN THE WOLVES FINISHED THE 2002–03 SEASON 51–31 and then won Games 2 and 3 against the defending NBA champion Los Angeles Lakers in the playoffs, it looked like the team might finally end its postseason losing streak. But the powerful Lakers came back to win the next three games and send the Wolves home early again.

Before the next season, the Wolves reshaped their roster, bringing in such players as swingman Latrell Sprewell, center Michael Olowokandi, and guards Fred Hoiberg and Sam Cassell. By the end of the season, this new pack of Wolves had put together a franchise-best 58–24 record and earned the team's eighth consecutive pass into the playoffs. Garnett proved himself as perhaps the NBA's most versatile star, averaging 24 points and almost 14 rebounds a game and capturing league Most Valuable Player (MVP) honors.

TIMBERWOLVES

At 7 feet tall and 270 pounds, Michael Olowokandi gave the Wolves much-needed size at the center position

27

The Wolves made the playoffs in eight of the nine full seasons that Flip Saunders paced the sidelines

NBA

The top-seeded Wolves made quick work of the Denver Nuggets in the first round. As Game 5 came to an end in the Wolves' favor, a fan threw a stuffed monkey onto the Target Center floor, symbolizing that the team had finally gotten the first-round playoff monkey off its back. "I'm very excited," Garnett said. "I'm not going to downplay it. I'm eager to see what is on the other side."

Round two turned into a thrilling, seven-game showdown between Minnesota and the Sacramento Kings. Minnesota fans were left ecstatic as the Wolves won Game 7 at home and advanced to face the star-studded Lakers in the Western Conference Finals. Unfortunately, an injury to Cassell hobbled the Wolves, and the Lakers won the series in six games.

The Minnesota faithful were ready for greater things the next season, but instead of moving forward, the 2004–05 Wolves slipped back. After a 25–26 start, longtime coach Flip Saunders was fired, and general manager Kevin McHale stepped in to finish the season. The team never completely recovered, finishing 44–38 and missing the postseason for the first time

A ROUND ON KG Before the Timberwolves took on the Phoenix Suns on February 14, 2002, Kevin Garnett made an offer that many Minnesota fans couldn't refuse. Garnett promised to buy a drink—either soda or beer—for the first 10,000 fans at the Target Center doors that evening, in hopes that people would both show up early and cheer loudly. A total of 18,701 fans showed up that night to watch the Wolves run over the Suns and former Timberwolves point guard Stephon Marbury 107–92. Although it cost the superstar forward around $15,000 to buy that round of drinks for the fans, Garnett was happy to follow through on his offer. "I thought it'd be a cool thing," he said. "I totally love our fans. This was my way of giving back to them."

since 1997. "Everybody is disappointed," McHale said. "You can't come into a year with the expectation level we had and have the type of season we had."

After the season, Wolves team officials set out to make the team more youthful and athletic. They took a step in that direction by selecting explosive, 6-foot-4 guard Rashad McCants with the team's top pick in the 2005 NBA Draft. They also believed they found the right man to lead the team from the bench, hiring longtime Seattle SuperSonics assistant Dwane Casey as the new head coach. Then, midway through the 2005–06 season, Minnesota shook things up further by trading away Wally Szczerbiak and Michael Olowokandi and bringing in athletic guard Ricky Davis.

Since 1989, Minnesota fans have spent many winter evenings watching stars such as Kevin Garnett gradually build the Timberwolves into an NBA power. The steps along the way have sometimes been painful, but the tough times have helped sharpen the focus of this dangerous team. With a little luck, today's Timberwolves will soon let out a championship howl.

31

Rashad McCants helped the University of North Carolina win the college national championship in 2005

TIMBERWOLVES

B

Basketball Hall of Fame 11

Brandon, Terrell 20, **21**

C

Campbell, Tony **9**, 11

Casey, Dwane 30

Cassell, Sam 26, 29

D

Davis, Ricky 30

G

Garnett, Kevin **4**, 5, 16, **17**, 19, **19**, 20,

    25, 26, 29, 30

Garrett, Dean 19

Gugliotta, Tom **14**, 15, 19, 20

H

Hoiberg, Fred 26

Hubert H. Humphrey Metrodome 11

L

Laettner, Christian 12, **13**, 15, 19

Lohaus, Brad 11

Lowe, Sidney 11, 15

M

Marbury, Stephon **18**, 19, 20

McCants, Rashad 30, **31**

McHale, Kevin 11, **11**, 16, 25, 29, 30

Minneapolis, Minnesota 8

Minnesota Timberwolves

    first season 11

    name 8

    team records 23, 26

Mitchell, Sam 11

Most Valuable Player Award 26

Musselman, Bill 11

N

NBA playoffs 19, 20, 23, 27, 29

NBA records 15

NBA Slam Dunk Contest 15

O

Olowokandi, Michael 26, **27**, 30

P

Person, Chuck ("The Rifleman") 12

R

Richardson, Jerome ("Pooh") **10**, 11

Rider, Isaiah 15, **15**

Rodgers, Jimmy 11, 12, 15

S

Saint Paul, Minnesota 8

Saunders, Phil ("Flip") 11, 17, **28**, 29

Sealy, Malik 23, 25, **25**

Smith, Joe 20, **22**, 23

Sprewell, Latrell 26

Stern, David 23

Szczerbiak, Wally 23, **24–25**, 30

T

Target Center 5, 11, 15, 29

Taylor, Glen 15

W

West, Doug 19

Williams, Michael 12